Contents

Foreword

Cabinet Office

I welcome the publication of this guidance by the Emergency Planning College (epc). Safety Advisory Groups are critical in assuring that public safety issues are central to the work of the events industry. They have an excellent track record and I have every confidence that the guidance contained here is a strong foundation for future practice. The fact that the Emergency Planning College has worked closely with partners in the entertainment and events industry and in government reflects its commitment to be at the heart of the public safety and resilience community, encouraging debate and reflection where it is needed, and leading the way for practitioners and policy makers in establishing and promoting good practice. I commend it to you and thank my colleagues at the Emergency Planning College for bringing it to you.

Dr Campbell McCafferty
Director
Civil Contingencies Secretariat, Cabinet Office

In his report into the Hillsborough Stadium Disaster, Lord Taylor recommended that local authorities should set up Safety Advisory Groups to assist them in exercising their functions under the Safety of Sports Grounds legislation. The Safety Advisory Group therefore fulfils an important role, and should be properly constituted with written terms of reference and effective procedures encompassing all matters falling within the local authority's regulatory duties. In 2009, the Sports Grounds Safety Authority published guidance on safety certification including the role, membership and management of the Safety Advisory Group.

With the increase in the number, variety and complexity of public events, from street parties to festivals, many local authorities now convene advisory groups for other types of activities that fall outside the legal framework for certificated sports grounds. This document seeks to provide guidance which could be applied to both types of advisory groups, reflecting the distinctive roles and status of each.

It is important that everyone involved in delivering spectator events understands the roles, responsibilities and liabilities. I hope you will find this guide interesting and useful, and wish you every success in the delivery of safe, secure and enjoyable events.

Ruth Shaw
Chief Executive
Sports Grounds Safety Authority

Endorsements

The Health and Safety Executive

The Health and Safety Executive (HSE) was consulted in the production of this guidance document. While the guidance goes beyond compliance with workplace health and safety law, it provides advice on the roles and responsibilities of those involved in non-statutory Safety Advisory Groups. For guidance on compliance with workplace health and safety law, you should refer to the HSE website at: http://www.hse.gov.uk/event-safety/safety-advisory-groups.htm

The College of Policing

The College of Policing is pleased to endorse the content of this, the first piece of national guidance on Safety Advisory Groups.

Clive Brooks
Head of Joint Operations
The College of Policing

Local Authority Events Organisers' Group

As Safety Advisory Groups came into existence and became adopted as good practice it was inevitable that local authorities would find their own ways to organise and operate them in their own areas. Though well-intentioned, this created inconsistencies between authorities, meaning that Safety Advisory Groups were sometimes used as an enforcement tool, thereby leaving event organisers crying out for guidance to help address the problem.

I am delighted that the Emergency Planning College has taken the lead role in doing this, carrying out comprehensive research and subsequently producing this guidance with considerable input and engagement from the industry. The guidance clearly sets out the role of the Safety Advisory Group, defining how it should be set up as well as identifying who should attend, what events should be considered by a Safety Advisory Group and what an organiser can expect when attending. The focus is now firmly back on the fact that it is an advisory group attended by competent personnel with a remit to focus on the quality assurance of event safety plans and offering sound safety advice to organisers.

I believe this excellent guidance will bring about changes that will lead to consistently positive and beneficial experiences for organisers and safer events for everybody. It has my full support.

Andy Grove
Chair
Local Authority Events Organisers' Group (LAEOG)

Association of Festival Organisers

The Association of Festival Organisers has always believed that Safety Advisory Groups are there to help festivals and events run smoothly. Throughout England there has been variation in how they operate and meet their brief.

We are delighted that the Emergency Planning College consulted widely with the industry to produce this guidance which we believe will be of benefit not only to the users but also to the wider events industry.

Steve Heap
General Secretary
Association of Festival Organisers

1. Aim of the guidance

1.1 This guidance is intended to form a single, core guidance document for Safety Advisory Groups (SAGs), their members, event organisers and others in the industry. It is also intended to act as a reference document that new or inexperienced event organisers might use in order to understand the structure, roles, responsibilities and expectations of a SAG.

1.2 The lack of regulation and legislation on SAGs has one distinct advantage. It means the SAG has no limitations as to what events it considers, should it so desire. It need not be restrained by venue (public or private); the arrangements (ticketed or unticketed); free or for payment; traditional or innovative; annual, monthly or exceptional; voluntary or charitable.

1.3 The guidance is not only a point of reference for all those with event safety roles; it has also been developed by using examples of good practice across the United Kingdom. Existing SAGs are encouraged to use it to confirm consistency with others, while those considering establishing a SAG can use it as a logical starting point.

1.4 It has been written from the outset as a guide and seeks to assist and support those aiming to follow good practice; it is not intended to be prescriptive.

1.5 An abbreviated version of the guidance will be available as a chapter within the Events Industry Forum's *Purple Guide*[1] and amendments to either document will be reflected in the other.

1.6 The purpose of a SAG, and certainly of this guidance, is to consider events in the context of their being essential to the communities of the UK. The SAG should examine the safety aspects of events so they can proceed in as safe a way as is reasonably practicable, ideally without compromising the public's enjoyment of them.

2. Background to Safety Advisory Groups

2.1 SAGs have been in existence for many years in relation to football events. Following the deaths of 66 people at Ibrox in 1971 (see Figure 1), Lord Wheatley reported extensively on safety matters and lessons to be learned. His report led to the Safety of Sports Ground Act (1975) which required local authorities, fire and police to consult in terms of the issue of safety certificates for football grounds.

2.2 Later, Lord Justice Taylor, while investigating the deaths of 96 spectators at the Hillsborough disaster in April 1989 (see Figure 1), referred to Lord Wheatley's findings. He specifically highlighted paragraph 67 of the *Report of the Inquiry into Crowd Safety at Sports Grounds*,[2] which stated: *'it can come as no surprise to the football world, and in light of happenings over the years, the demand for an independent appraisal and determination of the safety of grounds becomes almost irresistible. I certainly cannot resist it'.*

Figure 1 The Ibrox (left) and Hillsborough (right) stadium disasters prompted the establishment of Safety Advisory Groups

© Ibrox: Drew Innes; Hillsborough: Bev Griffiths

2.3 In paragraph 31 of the *Hillsborough Stadium Disaster Inquiry*,[3] published in 1990, Lord Justice Taylor recommended that, '*To assist the local authority in exercising its functions, it should set up an advisory group (if this has not already been done) consisting of appropriate members of its own staff, representatives of the police, of the fire and ambulance services and of the building authority. The advisory group should consult representatives of the club and of a recognised supporters' organisation on a regular basis. The advisory group's terms of reference should encompass all matters concerned with crowd safety and should require regular visits to the ground and attendance at matches. The advisory group should have a chair from the local authority, and effective procedures. Its resolutions should be recorded and it should be required to produce regular reports for consideration by the local authority*'.

2.4 The publication, followed by the regular updating, of the *Guide to Safety at Sports Grounds*[4] (commonly referred to as the *Green Guide*; see Figure 2), and establishment of the Football Licensing Authority (FLA; now the Sports Ground Safety Authority (SGSA)), have further contributed towards safety at football matches and have constantly re-emphasised the importance of SAGs.

Figure 2 The *Guide to Safety at Sports Grounds (Green Guide)*

2.5 In terms of musical events and others, no similar major disasters have occurred in the UK (although disasters have occurred overseas, and continue to do so). However, there have been some notable crowd-related incidents.

2.6 It is not widely known that crowd crushing at a David Cassidy concert in 1974 led to the death of 14-year-old Bernadette Wheelan, as well as causing hundreds of casualties.

2.7 In 1988 two people died, having been asphyxiated underfoot at the Monsters of Rock concert at Donington Park. This led directly to the development of the *Guide to Health, Safety and Welfare at Pop Concerts and Similar Events* in 1993. Subsequently this document was broadened in scope for a second edition with the title *The Event Safety Guide*, published in 1999. Now the Events Industry Forum has published what is formally known as the *Purple Guide*,[1] although the previous documents had informally been known by that name or sometimes as *The Pop Code*.

2.8 In the case of the Monsters of Rock tragedy, however, there was no public inquiry, and hence no equivalent of the FLA or SGSA, and no legislation was introduced, as was the case with Ibrox and Hillsborough. This remains the situation to date, despite incidents such as the two fatalities, and 193 other casualties, subjected to 'crushing' in Trafalgar Square in 1982, and two fatalities and many injuries to others as the result of the Dreamspace incident in Chester-le-Street in 2006.

2.9 It is acknowledged that the majority of events in the UK are planned and managed to high standards. However, 'near-misses' in crowd situations, and at public events, do occur but go unreported, meaning that opportunities for improvement pass unnoticed.

2.10 While there have been previous attempts to try to introduce national guidance on SAGs, these have met with only partial success. Many local authorities have established successful SAGs with their own local arrangements while others have chosen not to do so. In some cases there is an apparent concern that establishing such a group could incur a responsibility and culpability upon it.

2.11 Surveys regarding national SAG guidance undertaken by the Emergency Planning College (epc) in 2011 and 2012 received strong support for such a document from local authorities, emergency services and event organisers alike. Similarly, a national 'Working in Safety Advisory Groups' course, run since 2008 by the epc, has identified a strong desire for consistency in terms of SAG structures, terms of reference, membership, and roles and responsibilities. This desire must surely be best fulfilled in the form of national guidance.

2.12 This guidance document has therefore been written with all the above in mind, though only after extensive consultation throughout the sports and event industries. It can be considered as a summary of good practice for those within the public, private and voluntary elements of these industries who constantly strive to enhance public safety at events and maintain the UK's status as one of the safest countries in which to hold large and complex public festivals and events.

3. Safety Advisory Group constitutions

3.1 Introduction

3.1.1 Although the formation and retention of a SAG is not a legal requirement, SAGs are a good-practice model, as recommended in several of the key guidance documents, such as the *Purple Guide*.[1]

3.1.2 The SAG may be formed in relation to a specific event, venue or with a broader remit in relation to a range of events. It will, however, be important to ensure that what we will refer to as a 'constitution' exists. This should set out clearly the roles and responsibilities attaching to it, the membership, and the policies that may underpin how it is to function.

3.1.3 What should be vital is to ensure that a quality assurance process is in place in terms of the safety arrangements for events. While there may be alternative means of achieving this, such as third-party review, the option of having a SAG, comprising competent individuals and scrutinising the safety arrangements for an event, must be the preferred option.

3.2 Terms of reference

3.2.1 An important element of the constitution will be the terms of reference. These should accurately reflect the key role of providing a quality assurance process for the safety-related aspects for any event(s) and venue(s) falling within this role. It is stressed that the functions of this group should be distinct from those of the planning group for such events, and indeed it should not be confused with the arrangements for the management of the event(s) (see sections 3.7–3.8).

3.2.2 Agreeing these terms of reference is a matter for local determination. However, the following examples may assist in this process. These may be either generic or specific according to the nature of the role at this local level. Generic terms of reference may include:

- To promote clarity of roles and responsibilities relevant to the event(s) within the SAG's remit
- To advise the local authority and/or event organiser in order to ensure high standards of health and safety
- To promote the principles of sensible risk management and good practice in safety and welfare planning
- To promote a consistent, coordinated, multi-agency approach to event planning and management
- To advise the local authority and/or event organiser in respect of the formulation of appropriate contingency and emergency arrangements
- To advise the local authority and/or event organiser in respect of relevant legislation and guidance
- To encourage arrangements to be made to minimise disruption to local communities
- To consider the implications of significant incidents and events relevant to their venue(s) and events

- To consider the implications of significant incidents and events relevant to the surrounding areas and facilities
- To receive reports relevant to debriefs, visits and/or inspections of the venue or event.

3.2.3 In some cases it will be relevant to consider specific terms of reference in addition to these generic examples. These may include:

- To advise the local authority with regards to its functions in relation to safety certification
- To advise the local authority with regards to its powers under the licensing legislation.

3.2.4 In some cases it has been determined that a SAG will consider only certain categories of event, such as those on local authority land. Of course, the reality is that this could preclude consideration of other events that may involve higher levels of otherwise unrecognised risk, and such an approach is therefore to be discouraged.

3.2.5 Whatever terms of reference are agreed, it is good practice to ensure that all members of the group are aware of and generally in agreement with them. One way of achieving this is to include them on the agenda for meetings. Furthermore, it is good practice to review the terms of reference on an annual basis to ensure that they are still relevant.

3.3 Membership of the Safety Advisory Group

3.3.1 In his report, Lord Justice Taylor refers to statutory, non-statutory and invited members of a SAG. For the purpose of this guidance we will refer simply to core and invited members. Core members are expected to attend all meetings and all agenda items. Invitees may expect to be present only for particular meetings, agenda items or because they have specific experience that may benefit the group in relation to issues under discussion or consideration. Section 3.8 covers the format for meetings in more detail.

3.3.2 It will be important to ensure that members have the appropriate skills, experience, and position in their organisation to be credible and competent members of the group. Inexperienced, untrained or incompetent representatives may lead not only to unsafe decisions being made but, more likely, also put an excessive demand on event organisers to make events safe almost beyond what is reasonably practicable. The survey results, available from the epc library, show that there were many complaints from event organisers of unfair and unrealistic demands being placed upon them, normally by new and inexperienced SAGs or SAG members. These examples included SAG members making demands in areas far outside their own knowledge or their organisations' responsibilities. In order to ensure SAGs are not avoided by organisers, SAG members must be realistic and fair in their expectations and knowledge and experience among members is crucial.

3.3.3 Consideration must be given to the relevant organisations being involved in the group's processes in order for a suitable and sufficient review of event proposals to take place. If, for instance, a medical plan is to be reviewed, a representative from that background is required to support the quality assurance process. Equally, considering the basis for the calculation of safe capacities will require the involvement of member(s) competent in such issues. Figure 3 shows some examples of core members.

At county, district/borough, metropolitan and/or unitary levels it could include licensing, environmental health or others as appropriate on a local basis.

Local authority

Event management

Police service

Fire and rescue service

Health providers

Figure 3 Examples of core members of a Safety Advisory Group

All images © Shutterstock

Invited members may include, but are not limited to:

- Other local authority representatives as deemed appropriate – such as events team, emergency planning, highways, health and safety, communication/media, and legal services
- Event organisers/promoters
- Venue owners/operators
- Health boards
- Stewarding
- Security
- Traffic planners
- Transport providers
- British Transport Police
- Maritime and Coastguard Agency
- Medical
- Supporters' representation
- Resident/community representation
- Official bodies (e.g. Sports Ground Safety Authority)
- Highways Agency
- Crowd safety managers.

3.4   Chairing of the Safety Advisory Group

3.4.1   It is most common, though not always the case, for the chair of a group to be a representative appointed by the local authority. In some cases it has been determined that this person should be an independent appointee. What is vital, if the group is to function effectively and efficiently, is to have someone with the appropriate skills and competencies for this potentially demanding role. These are more likely to be competencies in communication, diplomacy and interpersonal skills than detailed legal or subject matter knowledge.

3.4.2 The chair should be able to absorb and evaluate the detailed arrangements for events while maintaining an objectivity of approach, taking into account the views of the group members.

3.4.3 In some cases the chair of the group may be in a position to make decisions on behalf of their authority. In such a case it is advisable that, where a devolved responsibility to the chair has been agreed, this is fully documented. It is also advisable that checks are made to ensure that professional indemnity insurance is in place in this respect.

3.4.4 It is stressed, however, that decisions taken in this way, such as in relation to licensing conditions, will be those of the authority and not the SAG, which is a purely advisory forum.

3.4.5 In many cases the chair of a group will not be a decision maker, and indeed the decision maker may not be present at meetings, or even be involved in the group processes. Where this applies it will be vital to ensure that a full and accurate account of the SAG representations is given to assist the decision maker's deliberations.

3.4.6 In many situations a SAG, chaired by a local authority representative, may be considering the arrangements for one of its own events. In such cases it is important to be able to demonstrate a transparency in the group's processes. It would be appropriate to avoid suggestions of bias by having the chair declare any conflict of interest if necessary, in order to avoid such allegations. Where such conflict exists, alternative chairing arrangements (preferably independent) should be made. Figure 4 shows the key responsibilities of the chair of the group.

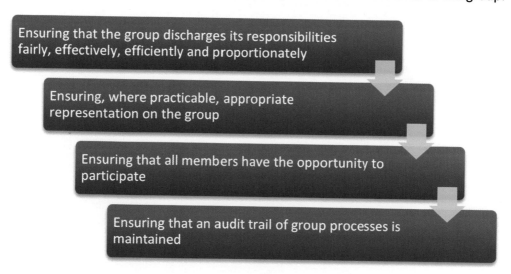

Figure 4 Responsibilities of the chair of a Safety Advisory Group
© Emergency Planning College

3.5 The roles and responsibilities of core members

3.5.1 Although there will be local variations, this section looks to identify the most relevant responsibilities applicable to core members. It should also be remembered that some of these operate across significant geographic authority areas, which may result in their being involved in numerous SAGs. This clearly emphasises the need to achieve consistency within the arrangements for such groups.

Event organisers

An event organiser's responsibilities will include all health and safety-related matters, as the two can be closely aligned. Health and safety responsibilities may include:

- Responsibilities towards employees
- Safe systems of work
- Arrangements to protect other persons
- Risk assessment
- Health and safety policy
- Method statement(s)
- Health and safety advice
- Monitoring
- Audit/record keeping
- Fire safety risk assessment.

Event safety

Event safety responsibilities may include:

- Event risk assessment
- Traffic/transport planning and management
- Crowd safety planning and management
- Security planning and management
- Emergency and contingency planning and management
- Medical/first aid planning and management
- Stewarding, planning and management
- Committing to agreeing a statement of intent
- Communication arrangements
- Welfare arrangements for the event
- Licensing, safety certification and other statutory requirements
- Ensuring appropriate insurance cover is in place
- Participation and cooperation with the SAG, including providing timely submission of appropriate event documentation.

Local authority

Depending upon the nature of the local authority, it:

- Will be a Category 1 responder under the Civil Contingencies Act
- Will be responsible for some matters related to health and safety and duty of care, including those of its own staff
- Will be an important member of the group
- May be the venue owner and/or operator
- May be the event organiser
- May be the lead authority for the issue, review, monitoring and enforcement of safety certification (for example, prohibition notices under the 1975 Safety at Sports Ground Act)

- May be the lead authority for the issue, review, monitoring and enforcement of licenses under the Licensing Act 2003
- May be the lead authority for environmental health matters
- May be responsible for highways management and maintenance
- May chair the group and/or be responsible for the appointment of the chair.

It should be remembered that some groups may involve more than one local authority, due to either geographic or organisational considerations. For example, in a two-tier arrangement, a safety certificate would be the responsibility of a county authority and a premises licence that of a district/borough authority.

Police service

The police service:

- Has statutory powers (see Appendix A)
- Is responsible for dealing with public order
- Has intelligence-gathering and coordination capabilities
- Responds to incidents where and when appropriate
- Is responsible for crime investigation and reduction
- Provides community policing
- Is responsible for health and safety and duty of care in respect of its staff
- Is an important member of the group
- Is a Category 1 responder under the Civil Contingencies Act.
- May provide policing, where applicable, for an event.

Fire and rescue service

The fire and rescue service:

- Is a Category 1 responder under the Civil Contingencies Act
- Has statutory powers and enforcement of standards (see Appendix A)
- Responds to incidents where and when appropriate
- Is responsible for health and safety and duty of care in respect of its staff
- Is an important member of the group
- May be the provider of fire safety resource.

Ambulance service

The ambulance service:

- Is a Category 1 responder under the Civil Contingencies Act
- Responds to incidents and emergencies
- Is responsible for health and safety and duty of care in respect of its staff
- Is an important member of the group
- May provide medical and first aid advice/assessment
- May be a medical provider.

Venue owner/operator

Even where the owner of the land or premises has no direct involvement with an event, other than providing the location, the venue owner or operator *may* still:

- Ensure that appropriate insurance cover is in place
- Ensure that only *bona fide* or authorised equipment is allowed on site

- Be responsible for establishing the extent of licensing requirements
- Fulfil general duties under health and safety legislation
- Obtain a fire safety risk assessment
- Ensure land and/or premises are in such a condition as not to cause danger to users and/or visitors (see Occupiers' Liability Act in Appendix A)
- Be an important member of the group.

3.6 Policy to underpin Safety Advisory Group procedures

3.6.1 There is often a fine line between what might be deemed to be part of the terms of reference and what could perhaps be better regarded as an underpinning policy. If we consider the terms of reference to be focused on *what* a SAG does, the policy may be deemed to be more about *how* this is done. Such a policy may include some of the following:

- It is the policy of the SAG to offer advice in order to ensure the highest possible standards of public safety at events and to encourage the wellbeing of those who could be affected by such events. In this context the 'public' includes not only those attending the event, but also those in the surrounding areas who may be affected by it.
- The SAG is not responsible for reviewing safe systems of work of the event organisation or crew. However, it will be relevant to consider the consequences of work-related incidents during periods of public access.
- The SAG does not make any decisions on behalf of the local authority or other agencies as its role is advisory and as such it has no authority to either approve or ban events.
- The decision-making authority is typically the local authority, which may be the chair of the SAG. Where other agencies may exercise their own statutory decision-making authority it is stressed that this is the determination of that authority and not of the SAG.
- The overall responsibility for the safety of persons at an event will lie with the event organiser, venue owner or operator and management team.
- Members of the SAG must declare any material conflict of interest in relation to any matters put before the group before any discussion on that matter. Should this conflict of interest be considered prejudicial, that person should consider withdrawing, to be replaced by an appropriate party agreed with the group.
- The SAG will have arrangements to ensure that appropriate records of procedures and meetings are maintained.
- The lessons learned via the SAG's processes and procedures will be applied for the benefit of all events within its area of responsibility.

3.7 When should a Safety Advisory Group consider an event?

3.7.1 This has been an area where there have been high levels of inconsistency between SAGs, as previously stated (see also section 3.2). For example, some will consider only events on local authority land, while others will have a broader perspective and use wider criteria. Many will consider events where the anticipated number of attendees exceeds a trigger figure. While this approach has some merit, **the levels of risk associated with an event may be greater with events that may not reach this trigger (the type of audience, for example, is equally important).**

3.7.2　It is important to develop a protocol that will assist in this process and safeguard those making these decisions in terms of their liabilities. Of course, referring an event to a SAG does not necessarily imply lengthy discussions at meetings as there are 'smarter' ways of discharging the responsibilities; these are covered in section 3.8.

3.7.3　Deciding whether to refer an event to a SAG requires a consistent methodology. This should always follow a risk-based approach, and should be determined by considering a combination of the factors shown in Figure 5.

Figure 5　Factors to consider when deciding whether to refer an event to a Safety Advisory Group
© Emergency Planning College

3.7.4　Many SAGs have developed protocols to assist in this process, some of which are identified in Appendix C. It will be important to identify who is to determine whether an event is referred to a SAG and to ensure that they are competent and confident to do so.

3.7.5　A SAG can consider only events of which it is aware. Many events will fall outside of the regulatory arrangements, such as licensing, and consequently will not necessitate formal notification. Members of a SAG should, however, ensure that there is a focal point at which details of events can be collated as soon as they are aware of them.

3.7.6　It should then be possible for an event organiser to be contacted in order to obtain further details on which to base the decision regarding referral to the SAG. This is quite easy to do and can be managed via local authority websites and online e-form facilities. Although the form may require only basic event and organiser details, it will inform the decision whether more detailed information is required.

3.7.7　SAGs will often have long-established relationships with event organisers and venues where degrees of trust and historical evidence have developed. There should, however, be no complacency in such cases, and indeed there should be a culture of seeking continual improvement. Where a SAG deals with unfamiliar events, organisers and venues, it will be particularly relevant for the SAG processes to be applied. Of course, a healthy measure of common sense and pragmatism must be involved but a protocol will provide the degree of consistency that is necessary in this process.

3.7.8 References to examples of e-forms and protocols are included in Appendix C.

3.7.9 It should be remembered that, while a single event may seem relatively insignificant in isolation, it may be one of several events occurring simultaneously, the combined effects of which would warrant SAG quality assurance processes.

3.7.10 SAGs may seek to apply a minimum period for notification of events, and some SAGs may apply a policy whereby they will not consider events falling outside of this period. While this is understandable, there is a risk that events falling below the appropriate standards of safety will not be subject to the necessary scrutiny. It will almost certainly be the case that such restrictions would not be supported in law when taken by a body with no statutory basis.

3.7.11 It must be remembered that for certain cases, such as 'tribute events', organisers will also be working within extremely tight deadlines. It will, however, be important to encourage cooperation from event organisers to ensure timely notifications and availability of relevant documentation. It is therefore important to seek to establish a culture whereby it is recognised that working with a SAG is positive and beneficial.

3.8 Safety Advisory Group processes and meetings

3.8.1 A robust SAG process will often provide an opportunity for a 'lighter touch' licensing process, particularly where the event organiser is cooperating. This is compatible with current government processes and thinking to support and encourage events to be organised within the UK as part of the 'big society' principles.

3.8.2 While historically SAGs have tended to review event arrangements at meetings, this can be time-consuming and involve significant travel and cost.

3.8.3 Many have therefore identified 'smarter' ways of working that can be more efficient and effective. Meetings will still have a part to play, however, and can have the added advantage of fostering relationships for future benefit.

3.8.4 There are now many technical options for the circulation of event documentation such as file transfer protocol (FTP) sites, where their use does not breach local protocols. It is therefore good practice to use such options to circulate documentation to SAG members.

3.8.5 The onus must then be on SAG members to review the documentation and to raise any issues of concern, advice and so forth. If no such concerns are raised it will not normally be necessary to discuss the matter at a meeting. Indeed, even where concerns have been raised, it may be possible to resolve them without the need for a meeting. This approach relies on SAG members taking their own responsibilities seriously during the review process.

3.8.6 Many members would need to travel considerable distances to attend a meeting. Event organisers, and others, may be dealing with extremely high volumes of events, restricting their ability to attend all meetings. Consideration should therefore be given to the appropriate use of telephone or videoconferencing as an alternative. These options would enable members to participate remotely.

3.8.7 Forming subgroups can work well, especially for large-scale or complex events. This can sometimes be a more effective and efficient means of fulfilling the processes. It will be necessary to ensure that there is overarching coordination of the subgroups.

3.8.8 As SAG members will have many other responsibilities, it is important to ensure that meetings are held only as necessary, and that best use is made of people's time.

3.8.9 When and where to hold meetings will depend on the nature of the SAG. Where it is venue-specific there will almost certainly be advantages to holding meetings at that venue. The same may also apply to an event-specific SAG. The situation with a 'general-purpose' SAG is less clear; however, because it may deal with specific venues among its range of events, it is important for members to be familiar with those venues.

3.8.10 Meetings may be held on three bases: periodically; at specific points in the development of events; and/or as necessary owing to specific concerns and issues. An obvious example would be the relevance of a SAG for a football stadium meeting when the fixtures for the forthcoming season are announced.

3.8.11 Some SAG chairs have made arrangements to plan monthly meetings on, for example, a 'first Thursday' or 'last Tuesday' basis, as this enables core members to diarise them months or even years in advance. This can be done only when all members agree and where other regular meetings do not clash.

3.8.12 A general-purpose SAG may schedule meetings so that the various event organisers are allocated times when their own event is to be discussed. It should therefore not be necessary for all invitees to sit though discussions that are not relevant to them. There may also be issues of a commercially sensitive nature that would make it appropriate to restrict access.

3.8.13 The chair of the group should ensure that the meeting runs efficiently, and attendees should ensure they are well prepared for the meeting.

3.9 Administration of Safety Advisory Groups

3.9.1 Member organisations are currently experiencing considerable pressure on both finances and resources, so there will be inevitable implications for the administration arrangements of SAGs. This will be eased by event organisers and members each playing their part. It is normal for administrative responsibilities to be undertaken by the same organisation as the chair (typically the local authority), although this is not always the case.

3.9.2 Responsibilities will include being a conduit for information; communication; and coordination/distribution of documentation. Experience suggests that these requirements should not be underestimated. It is also vital to ensure that an audit trail is maintained reflecting the SAG processes.

3.9.3 Administrative work will include the preparation and circulation of agendas in advance of meetings, the referral processes of event proposals to SAGs, and the recording and circulation of resolutions and minutes of meetings. Given the importance of the chair's role, it will not be appropriate for them to record the minutes, so another member will need to be responsible for this. Ideally secretarial support will be provided by a person who is not a participating active SAG member.

3.9.4 The audit trail of a SAG will most certainly be the subject of public record, potential freedom of information application and any subsequent court proceedings, criminal or civil.

3.9.5 The SAG must have a process to avoid the unnecessary sharing of information outside the SAG that is commercially sensitive to the companies who own it. Some protection in this regard is provided by S43(2) of the Freedom of Information Act 2000 which states: *'Information is exempt information if its disclosure under this Act would, or would be likely to, prejudice the commercial interests of any person (including the public authority holding it'*. As such, any emails, plans or other similar documentation provided to the SAG and held by its members that is marked appropriately by the authors or requested to be treated as commercially sensitive should be withheld even if subject to requests under the Act.

4. Options and limitations of the Safety Advisory Group

4.1 As stated in section 3.6.1, SAGs as an entity have no bespoke powers although some have tended to resort to the powers of their individual members if legislative or enforcement action is necessary. It is important to stress again that the SAG is not an enforcement body. Whether or not an individual agency determines to resort to use of its own powers must be a decision for that agency and not the SAG. In reality, almost all SAG matters are resolved informally through negotiated processes.

4.2 The SAG would be likely to discuss the powers of its members when faced with an event that caused it concern for public safety. However, the members should not put pressure on others to use powers they would not otherwise implement.

4.3 As the SAG has no legislative power, the number of options available to it is limited. That said, any advice offered by a SAG that comprises competent members would most likely be highly influential in most cases and would certainly have an influence on any legal process.

4.4 While a SAG may advise in relation to the introduction and/or variation of conditions relating to safety certification and/or licensing, it is stressed that it should not be seen as a 'lobbying forum' in these respects.

4.5 SAG members may feel it appropriate to give advice regarding land usage permission where there are significant safety concerns that cannot be otherwise addressed. An example of this is where the local authority (or any member of the SAG) is in a position where an event on its land controlled is the subject of safety concerns. This advice could relate to the Occupiers' Liability Act(s) whereby the local authority would have a potential duty of care to those who will use the land as a worker, spectator or participant. Handing over control of the land to an event organiser would not relinquish this liability in its entirety (or possibly at all, if the local authority is aware of any deficiencies on the part of the organiser and fails to act).

4.6 While there may be no apparent legal duty to do so, some authorities and SAG members might consider there is a moral and ethical duty to inform a private landowner of significant safety concerns that they deem to pose a threat to public safety and the likely implications of these for the owner of the land.

4.7   Such a decision should not be taken lightly; it will be subject to close scrutiny at the time and potentially even more so at a later date, possibly in court if actions are taken by organisers who incur financial losses. While such a decision may have been subject to discussion and advice within the SAG, it is again stressed that this decision would have been taken by that member or organisation and not the SAG itself.

4.8   Cases such as these can result in public and media interest, particularly in relation to a historic, traditional or community event. This can sometimes be reported as a SAG 'banning' an event, but the SAG itself has no legal basis on which to do so. It is more often a case of land use permissions being withdrawn after the landowner has been made aware of the safety implications.

4.9   A SAG may sometimes wish to examine the insurance arrangements for an event. However, there is no legal requirement for these to be provided, nor is there a legal requirement for an event organiser to obtain public liability insurance.

4.10   However, where a local authority is in control of the land on which an event is to take place, it will certainly be prudent for it to check its insurance policies and to confirm that the activities being undertaken are covered.

4.11   A major challenge for a SAG is where an event organiser refuses to engage with it. Where a SAG becomes aware of an event which by its nature would normally be subject to the SAG process, the SAG should persevere in its attempts to establish contact with the organiser and details of all such attempts should be documented. This may involve contacting landowners and checking websites for organisers' details, ticket sale points, etc. First contact should seek to explain that the role of the SAG is as a supportive body and does not intend to prevent or curtail activity.

4.12   If the organiser refuses to engage with a SAG process, in whatever format, the SAG should consider why this is and whether there may be mitigating circumstances, such as travelling distances or involvement in other events.

4.13   The government has recognised the valuable contribution that events make to the UK and has encouraged them to be supported and allowed to take place subject to appropriate levels of safety. Where an event organiser declines to engage in safety processes, this will be challenging, but should not prevent the SAG taking reasonable steps to review the safety arrangements of the event.

4.14   A SAG process does not need to be lengthy or adversarial. Face-to-face meetings can be replaced by telephone calls, videoconferences or email, especially when organisers are attempting to arrange events in many locations at the same time.

4.15   A resolution may sometimes be better obtained away from large meetings and where a less formal approach is taken.

5. Exceptional circumstances

5.1 In the absence of specific written guidance on establishing, running and maintaining SAGs, many local authorities (and in some cases police or fire and rescue services) have established groups to consider the safety aspects of events within their area. While this is not to be recommended, some have gone further and formed joint groups that plan events, or contribute towards their planning. In some cases these groups have been necessitated by circumstances related to specific events, normally of a historic nature, where responsibility for organisation is unclear and therefore detailed planning and safety aspects have been, at best, questionable.

5.2 In such cases authorities have been left with little choice other than to face a threat to public safety if they do not take some action to assist in planning the event. Nonetheless, event organisers and communities should be encouraged to begin to undertake the planning functions and permit the local authority and SAG to undertake their roles to examine the safety aspects.

5.3 While the concept of joint groups leading on planning events is not desirable, it can be understandable in extreme circumstances. Notting Hill Carnival has a history of instances of considerable disorder and as such, has required high levels of policing towards the end of each day. As well as avoiding such public disorder, police involvement in planning aims to help organisers plan safer events in the future. Other agencies, such as local authorities, ambulance service, fire and rescue service and the Greater London Authority (as a principal funder) would also benefit from having input in planning certain aspects of the event, as they would have suffered the consequences of any disorder.

5.4 Some historical events also require, and in some cases are given, more assistance than might appear 'normal' in the modern concept where organisers are completely responsible for the public safety aspects of their event.

5.5 Figure 6 shows some examples of traditional or historic events that form part of the UK's culture. Most people agree such events should be supported, although not at the expense of public safety.

Figure 6 Safety is paramount at traditional and historic events such as Tar Barrels (left) and Lewes Bonfire (right)

Tar Barrels © Robert Chandler, Appendix B; Lewes Bonfire © Select Security and Stewarding Ltd, Brighton

5.6 There are, however, distinct differences between those events where participants of their own volition endanger themselves through an activity (for example, cheese rolling), and those where public spectators may be endangered through the activities of the participants (for example, Lewes Bonfire, where strong winds and close proximity to burning torches, along with thrown fireworks, led to a number of eye injuries in 2011).

5.7 Appropriate arrangements should therefore be in place to minimise the risk to participants, to ensure they are aware of such risk, and to ensure that appropriate responses are in place. For many events, such as soccer, boxing and cycle racing, official bodies will provide the arrangements for participants. Other organisers, such as the Scout Association and the British Council of Shopping Centres, have overseeing bodies that control the general activities of their members. In other cases, however, an external organiser may be responsible for the safety arrangements for both spectators and participants.

5.8 While we should expect arrangements for general public safety to be scrutinised, it is also crucial that the arrangements for participants are subject to similar examination. This is particularly so where participants may be unaware of the levels of risk they might be exposed to and assume that organisers have undertaken adequate preparation. These arrangements may be the responsibility of others, such as sporting bodies, but it will be vital to ensure that they are also considered by those involved in planning the event.

5.9 One example of inadequate safety arrangements was a sea swimming event at Southwold, Suffolk in 2013. This resulted in a potential threat to life when scores of participants got into difficulties owing to a delayed start and turning tide.

6. Conclusion

6.1 This guide ends, as it began, with a summary of some of the fundamental principles of the SAG process:

- Events are an important part of the lives of UK residents and should be encouraged.
- The UK government supports and encourages events, especially those organised by the community for the community.
- SAGs are a good means to examine the safety aspects of events and should be encouraged to do so.
- SAGs should be seen by organisers as supportive of their endeavours.
- There is no legal basis for SAGs to exist, although aspects of the Civil Contingencies Act may be deemed to make them so (see Appendix A).
- SAG members themselves may have legislative and enforcement powers.
- SAG membership should consist of experienced, competent practitioners.
- SAGs are advisory and have no power either to 'authorise' or 'ban' events.

Appendix A   Summary of relevant legislation

The legislation listed below is available at: www.legislation.gov.uk

A.1   General

As previously stated, current government policy strongly supports local and community events. According to the Live Music Exchange,[5] the events industry as a whole was worth in excess of £36 billion in 2012.

A SAG in itself has no regulatory powers. Much of the historical criticism of SAGs has been to do with their perceived lack of democratic status and their suggested focus on prevention of events rather than support for them. As SAGs have no statutory status in law their emphasis is as much on 'advisory' as it is on 'safety'. There is no legal requirement to hold a SAG meeting, nor for organisers or any of its members, to attend it. It should, however, be noted that duties and responsibilities under the Civil Contingencies Act/Framework should be a strong incentive for Category 1 responders to cooperate with each other in a SAG process held locally, particularly for what may be considered to be higher-risk events.

Despite this apparent lack of legislative power, there are options open to individual SAG members in terms of their own statutory powers and duties. These powers can, and should, be considered where it is necessary and appropriate to protect the public from harm so that all parties can show that they have paid due diligence and discharged their duties of care. Appendix B references some of these statutory responsibilities but the main legal powers are outlined below.

While a SAG can discuss and possibly advise in relation to these powers, the exercise of them will be entirely a matter for the agency and not the SAG.

A.2   Legislation

The following is a summary of primary legislation that a SAG might consider as relevant in relation to event safety proposals.

A.3   Licensing Act 2003

This Act is principal among these powers. Amended guidance under Section 182 of the Act was issued in June 2013 that re-emphasised the requirement for agencies to have a clear focus on 'the promotion of the key licensing objectives':

- The prevention of crime and disorder
- Public safety
- The prevention of public nuisance
- The protection of children from harm
- (Scotland only – protecting and improving public health).

It states that each of the above is of equal importance and must be addressed when licensing functions are undertaken.

Licensing authorities are duty bound to take all such matters into consideration in the granting of a licence for any such licensable activity.

The following types of licences can be obtained: personal, premises, club premises and temporary event notices (for events of 499 persons or fewer).

'Responsible authorities' have powers under Section 51 of the Act to seek a review of a licence on any of the grounds of the licensing objectives, including public safety.

Police have additional powers under Section 53A of the Act if alcohol is available for sale and a senior police officer believes that the premises are involved with serious crime or serious disorder (or both).

A police inspector or officer of higher rank may order a closure under Section 161 of the Act if he or she has a reasonable belief that there is, or is imminently likely to be, disorder on, or in the vicinity of and related to, the premises and their closure is necessary in the interests of public safety.

Many events, however, fall outside the Licensing Act 2003 and may not be subject to the normal scrutiny of a licensing panel. Such events include processions, parades, street carnivals and some performances of unamplified live music between 8 am and 11 pm, as amended by the Live Music Act 2012.

A.4   Licensing Act (Scotland 2005)

As mentioned above, the Licensing Act (Scotland) 2005 broadly replicates most of the 2003 Act with the addition of the fifth objective detailed in the last bullet point in A.3.

A.5   Licensing (Northern Ireland) Order 1996

Although there was consultation regarding the review of licensing legislation, this met with strong opposition and is not currently proceeding. It would have brought arrangements more into line with those in Great Britain. The situation is therefore much as it used to be in Great Britain, with 12 different forms of premises licence. Licensing applications are dealt with via the courts as opposed to local authorities in Great Britain. Although they may not fall under licensing regulation, this does not mean that partners in a SAG process cannot scrutinise events for public safety.

A.6   The Civil Contingencies Act 2004

This legislation places a duty on all Category 1 responders to 'assess the risk of emergencies occurring, to use this to inform emergency planning' and to 'put in place emergency plans'. Category 1 responders include: the emergency services, local authorities, Environment Agency, Maritime and Coastguard Agency and health authorities. They are responsible for undertaking such risk assessments within their area of responsibility and clearly this could include events and venues (such as stadiums and arenas), at which it could be reasonably foreseeable that such emergencies might occur.

In assessing risks, Category 1 responders might reasonably expect to work together to assess the risk of an event within their area, and take whatever steps are deemed appropriate, necessary and lawful to prevent emergencies occurring or be in a position to respond should an emergency occur.

The Civil Contingencies Act may therefore be considered a driver to assess the safety of events and a SAG is the appropriate means by which to do so.

An emergency might not only affect an event, and those attending it, but it could also have an impact on others in the vicinity. This could, for instance, include traffic congestion in a nearby village, delayed emergency response times or significant on-site casualties impacting on ambulance and hospital provision for residents of nearby towns or cities. An event may also be affected by an emergency or incident occurring in the immediate vicinity and aspects of negative impact in each direction between the event and the local community should be included in considerations.

The Civil Contingencies Act only partially applies in Northern Ireland with only the Police Service of Northern Ireland and MCA as Category 1 responders and telecommunications organisations as Category 2 (supporting organisations). However, the Civil Contingencies Framework does require other public bodies, such as local authorities, to apply the principle of the Civil Contingencies Act.

A.7 The Regulatory Reform (Fire Safety) Order 2005
This important legislation gives enforcement authorities statutory powers to issue alterations, enforcement or prohibition notices as it deems necessary. Details of enforcement authorities are given in Article 25 of the legislation. The powers relate to workplaces or premises, the notable exception being domestic premises. One key feature of this legislation is that the responsibility for fire safety is clearly identified as that of a responsible person for the relevant workplaces or premises in question.

A.8 The Fire (Scotland) Act 2005
This Act is broadly similar to the legislation cited in A.7.

A.9 Fire and Rescue Services (Northern Ireland) Order 2006 and the Fire Safety Regulations (Northern Ireland) 2010
Part 3 of the legislation came into effect on 15 November 2010. This simplified existing fire safety legislation in non-domestic premises and reinforced the modern risk-based approach to fire prevention. This again broadly replicates the legislation in Great Britain and similarly identifies the employers, and those with a degree of control, as responsible for reducing risk of fire and ensuring means of escape.

A.10 The Fire and Safety of Places of Sport Act 1987
This legislation covers the regulation of spectator stands with a roof and a capacity of 500 or more spectators at non-designated sports grounds. In such a case the safety certificate is applicable only to the stand or stands in question, and not the entire venue as with a general safety certificate.

A.11 Building Act 1984
Sections 77 and 78 of the Act give local authorities the power to apply to a magistrate for an order to ensure the owner of a building or structure makes it safe within a given period (Section 77) or, if there is immediate danger, they may take such steps as is necessary to remove the danger (Section 78). It states: 'If it appears to a local authority that a building or structure, or part of a building or structure, is in such a condition, or is used to carry such loads, as to be dangerous'. Loads might be considered to include persons. The definition given is of 'any permanent or temporary building and any other permanent or temporary structure, or erection, of whatever kind or nature'. Dependent upon the specific detail in question this could be applicable to temporary demountable structures at event sites.

The power also relates to vehicles of any nature (Section 121).

A.12 The Health and Safety at Work Etc. Act 1974 (Applicable by Order in Northern Ireland)

The Health and Safety at Work Act 1974 ('the Act') and the regulations made under it apply to duty-holders. The law requires them to do what is reasonably practicable to ensure health and safety. The Act sets out the general duties that employers have towards their employees. It also requires employers and the self-employed to protect people other than those at work (for example, volunteer staff and spectators) from risks to their health and safety arising out of, or in connection with, their work activities. You need to do a risk assessment only if you are an employer or a self-employed person. If you have fewer than five employees you do not have to keep a written record, but it is good practice to do so.

Health and safety law does not, generally, impose duties upon someone who is not an employer, self-employed or an employee; for example, a group of volunteers organising a street party. However, anyone (including volunteers) with control of non-domestic premises, such as a school or community hall, has legal responsibilities under health and safety law to make the premises and any equipment or substances provided for their use there safe, as far as is 'reasonably practicable'.

A.13 The Health and Safety (Enforcing Authority) Regulations 1998

This is an Act to outline those aspects of health and safety legislation that can be enforced by the HSE or by local authorities (or both).

A.14 Safety of Sports Grounds Act 1975

This legislation is applicable to open-air sport venues (whether a sliding roof is present or not) with a capacity of 5,000 or more for football or, 10,000 or more for other sports. At the current time the Secretary of State has determined that this will be a requirement only in relation to football, rugby and cricket sports grounds, although there is one example of an athletic stadium having opted to be so certificated. The legislation requires the issue of general safety certificates by local authorities relating to the activities that take place within it and relevant conditions (for example, capacities). It also covers the issuing of special safety certificates for events not covered by the general safety certificate, such as a pop concert at a football stadium.

Section 10 of the Act also permits the issuing of prohibition notices at any sports ground, even if is not so 'designated'. A prohibition notice could be issued if the local authority thought there was a serious risk to the admission of spectators. Issuing a prohibition notice could restrict the numbers of spectators to the whole or part of the sports ground; to zero in an extreme case.

A.15 Safety of Sports Grounds (Northern Ireland) Order 2006

This legislation broadly mirrors the above Sports Ground Acts of 1975 and 1987. It is relevant to note, however, that the designated capacity is 5,000 and the legislation is not limited to football, rugby and cricket as is the case in Great Britain.

A.16 Football-specific legislation

Considerable football-specific legislation exists including The Football Spectators Act 1989 (all seating at certain stadiums) and The Football (Offences) Act 1991 (missiles, obscene chanting and pitch incursion legislation). This guidance must assume detailed knowledge of all such football-related powers by those charged with dealing directly with these specific matters. As such the guide does not detail each piece of legislation.

A.17 Public Health Acts Amendment Act 1890

Section 37 of this little-known, and rather dated, legislation states that whenever large numbers of people are likely to assemble, any structure intended to be used for spectators must be safely constructed and secured to the satisfaction of the 'proper officer of the authority'. It makes it an offence for any person to use any unsafe structure, or allow it to be used by others.

A.18 Fireworks Regulations 2004 and Fireworks (Scotland) Regulations 2004

This legislation introduced the classification of fireworks into four categories, making possession of certain types illegal. It also legislates against the anti-social use of fireworks and use of fireworks outside of permitted hours.

A.19 The Explosive (Fireworks) Regulations (Northern Ireland) 2002

More controlling regulations based upon due consideration of historic misuse of fireworks in protest situations in Northern Ireland.

A.20 The Private Security Industry Act 2001

Among other elements this legislation also has the effect of imposing requirements for the training and licensing of security staff, and those involved in licensable roles (with exceptions) and CCTV operators including sport- and event-related staff in certain roles.

A.21 Occupiers' Liabilities Acts 1958 and 1984

The 1958 Act requires the occupiers of premises (generally interpreted as also applying to those in control of premises), to take reasonable steps so that persons entering the premises are kept reasonably safe. The 1984 Act extended the first to also include protection for trespassers into those premises.

A.22 Equalities Act 2010

Businesses are required to take reasonable steps to tackle physical features that could inhibit access to businesses, goods, facilities or services by those to whom the Act applies. This extends far beyond physical disability and includes gender reassignment, pregnancy and maternity, race, religion, belief and sexual orientation. While the SAG may have no requirement to scrutinise compliance with the Act, it may wish to consider whether adequate provision for safety and evacuation has been considered in relation to those attending with such additional 'needs'.

A.23 Corporate Manslaughter and Corporate Homicide Act 2007

This Act specifically aims to prosecute organisations, rather than individuals within it, in the event of a death caused by what amounts to a gross breach of a relevant duty of care owed by the organisation to the deceased. In such a case the company can receive unlimited fines. If a SAG is operating within its advisory remit it is unlikely that there would be any associated liabilities under this legislation, although there could be for other member organisations in extreme circumstances.

A.24   Gross Negligence Manslaughter (common law)

This is generally defined as failure to exercise a reasonable level of precaution given the circumstances and so may include both acts and omissions. This is important to note, because although it is untested in law (as far as we are aware), an omission or failing to undertake a safety review, assess risks under the Civil Contingencies Act, or other legislation, that was shown to lead directly to a death, might be regarded as a sufficient omission to be considered as failure to exercise such a reasonable level of care.

A.25   Criminal Justice and Public Order Act 1984 (as amended by the Anti-social Behaviour Act 2003)

This Act gives police powers to take action against illegal activities, such as raves and mass trespasses, and against those attending. These are police powers but might be discussed at SAGs in relation to potential illegal activities.

A.26   Crime and Disorder Act 1998

This legislation gives local authorities, police and some other agencies specified a *'duty to consider crime and disorder implications'*. Specifically the Act states that: *'Without prejudice to any other obligation imposed on it, it shall be the duty of each authority to which this section applies to exercise its various functions with due regard to the likely effect of the exercise of those functions on, and the need to do all that it reasonably can to prevent, crime and disorder in its area'*. A licensing authority must have due regard to the implications of an event it is considering, just as a local authority landowner should do likewise before agreeing the use of its land.

A.27   The Public Order and Criminal Justice (Scotland) Act 2006

A complex piece of legislation which, as well as covering the establishment of the Scottish Police Services Authority, also covers issues such as those relating to public processions, football-banning orders, offensive weapons and possession of prohibited fireworks.

A.28   Road-specific legislation

A considerable amount of road-specific legislation is in force that permits the closure of roads under certain circumstances. In London Section 52 of the Metropolitan Police Act 1839 still empowers officers using 'commissioners' directions' to close roads, though this is used more and more sparingly. Outside London similar powers are available under the Town and Police Clauses Act 1847 and are used varyingly across the UK.

Road closure powers are also available under Section 16a Road Traffic Regulations 1984, although there are often significant charges that accompany such closures, which vary widely across the UK.

Section 115 of the Highways Act 1980 gives councils powers to place structures, stalls, etc. on highways.

The Cycle Racing on Highways Regulations 1960 (Amended 1980 and 1995) sets out the requirements of organisers to ensure certain restrictions are placed on such races and authorises roads to be used for such if those conditions are met.

The Traffic Management Act 2004 directs local authorities to:

- Identify things (including future occurrences) that are causing, or that have the potential to cause, road congestion or other disruption to the movement of traffic on their road network; and
- Consider any possible action that could be taken in response to (or in anticipation of) anything so identified.

This legislation has been considered for use by some authorities as a means to discussing traffic and parking arrangements for events that might impact on their transport network.

Note: Where the closure or a partial closure of a local street, such as a cul-de-sac or one requiring no diversions are concerned, the government's *Organising a Voluntary Event: a 'Can Do' Guide*[6] encourages councils to assist communities to carry these out with as little cost or administrative burden as possible.

A.29   Other legislation and devolved administrations

This guidance cannot cover all relevant legislation, but SAGs should ensure that they have access to the necessary knowledge and interpretation of such legislation including that which may relate to devolved administrations.

Some legislation in Scotland and Northern Ireland differs significantly from that in England and Wales. In some cases legislation is only partly enacted in one or other of the countries and in other cases specific legislation is in place.

This guidance therefore assumes that readers anywhere in the UK will have working knowledge of the legislation applicable in their own country, or failing that, access to such working knowledge.

Appendix B   Statutory responsibilities of Safety Advisory Group members

Not all SAG members will have statutory powers and responsibilities. In addition to issues covered in Appendix A the following may be relevant to a SAG:

- **Sports Grounds Safety Authority (SGSA)** Under the provisions of Part 1 of Football Spectators Act 1989 the SGSA operates a Licensing Scheme in respect of the viewing accommodation of Premier and Football League grounds in England and Wales. The role extends to the reviewing of how local authorities discharge their functions in relation to safety certification. The SGSA is the author of the *Guide to Safety at Sports Grounds*,[4] and the Sports Grounds Safety Authority Act 2011 extended its role to include the provision of advice and guidance on any event held at any sports ground.

- **Local Authority Environmental Health Officers (EHOs)** For the most part, EHOs will be responsible for enforcing the Health and Safety at Work Act 1974 and its subsidiary regulations at events, unless it is a local authority event, in which case HSE will be the enforcing authority. Together they ensure that duty-holders manage the risks to their staff and those affected by work activities.

- **Maritime and Coastguard Agency (MCA)** MCA has delegated responsibility for maritime search and rescue, among other roles and responsibilities. It also has authority in relation to coordination of response to maritime emergencies. As such it will be an obvious stakeholder in relation to events that are maritime in nature, such as sea swimming and yachting events.

- **British Transport Police (BTP)** BTP polices Britain's railways, providing a service to rail operators, their staff and passengers across the country. It also polices the London Underground, Docklands Light Railway, the Midland Metro tram system, Croydon Tramlink, Sunderland Metro, Glasgow Subway and Emirates Air Line. For events impacting upon these travel options BTP may be included in SAG arrangements or be represented by local police forces.

- **Highways Agency (HA)** Under the Traffic Management Act 2004, HA has the power to stop and direct traffic, close lanes and carriageways and manage traffic on the strategic roads network. These were responsibilities previously associated with policing. As such it will be appropriate to invite the HA onto a SAG where events will impact upon this network.

- **Sport Northern Ireland (Sport NI)** Works in partnership with Department of Culture, Art and Leisure to deliver on sport in Northern Ireland. In many respects this is a similar role to SGSA.

- **The Health and Safety Executive (HSE)** Has enforcement responsibility for the following work activities at all events – construction work covered by schedule 2(4) of the Health and Safety (Enforcing Authority) Regulations 1998, radio and television broadcasting and fairgrounds. In certain circumstances, arrangements can be made to transfer enforcement responsibilities between the HSE and local authorities. Further information about how the HSE and local authorities work together is available at: http://www.hse.gov.uk/lau/index.htm

Appendix C   Examples of good practice for Safety Advisory Groups

SAG members should be cautious about the use of the expression 'best practice' but could certainly suggest some examples of 'good practice' relative to SAGs and the way they function. Readers of this guidance may wish to consider some of the examples below when establishing or seeking to maintain good practice for SAGs.

Some local authorities have developed a risk-based scoring system for events to make decisions regarding application of the SAG processes. This approach is useful to avoid suggestions of impropriety within the SAG, as once a score is reached then the process would be applied regardless of the event or the applicant. It could be applied to both internal and external applications, so that the local authority scrutinises its own events to the same standard as external ones.

While this guidance is supportive of such arrangements in principle, it also suggests that this style of 'scoring' should be treated with some caution and applied only by those with some reasonable depth of event experience. Should an authority 'cut and paste' such a scoring system, without having had its own discussions as to the appropriate scores applied to each area, it would be potentially vulnerable to criticism by organisers and those reviewing event processes at a later stage. The only means of properly considering events is to take a risk-based methodology and apply it to each individual aspect of the event, venue and organiser.

County Durham Safety Advisory Group
Provides detailed guidance for event organisers as well as good examples of the questionnaires that organisers are required to complete in order that an assessment for referral to SAG can be undertaken. This is available at:

http://www.durham.gov.uk/article/3720/Events-safety-information-for-organisers

Stockton-on-Tees Borough Council
Offers guidance for event organisers, along with an initial event notification e-form, which is available at:

http://events.stockton.gov.uk/plan-an-event/

East Lindsey (Lincolnshire)
Has an established Event Safety partnership scheme which runs an event Safety Advisory Group through these channels. It offers advice, guidance and notification forms through its website. These are all readily available at:

http://www.e-lindsey.gov.uk/article/2020/Event-Organisation

Kent Police
Has a simple, one-page guidance sheet to Safety Advisory Groups in Kent which is available at:

http://www.kent.police.uk/advice/events/managing_events/sag.html

Lincolnshire Event Safety Partnership

Provides a strategic framework of consistent advice to local events Safety Advisory Groups across Lincolnshire to enable them to provide proportionate, timely and accurate guidance to event organisers. Comprehensive guidance and documentation is available at:

http://www.lincolnshire.gov.uk/lincolnshire-prepared/Lincolnshire-Event-Safety-Partnership

Appendix D   Questions and answers

D.1   What can be done where a key organisation refuses to support the SAG?

Where such non-engagement occurs, there are limited options for those who do engage to try to 'force' others to participate. There are some occasions where those declining to engage are from the statutory agencies of local authority, fire, police or ambulance, although these instances are unusual. It is, however, clear from surveys, epc courses and questions raised during and after these, that this does occur and is likely to do so even more often as budgets are restricted to the public services.

In these cases it is a matter for other partner agencies to discuss their options. These might include reminding the reluctant agency of its duties under legislation such as the Civil Contingencies Act; these are outlined in Appendix A.

Because SAGs are recommended in several of the key guidance documents, if an agency chose not to participate it would need to consider how it could justify the decision in the event that it were called to account.

We would hope that a SAG that operates effectively and efficiently would provide a strong encouragement for all key members to participate.

D.2   What can be done where an event organiser refuses to engage with the SAG?

As already stated, SAGs have no statutory power, and it is evident from the very start of the process that a SAG cannot demand that an event organiser participate or attend meetings. It is important to consider why an organiser is unwilling or unable to engage. It will be important to demonstrate that a SAG is well intentioned and focused on working with organisers, by considering the safety aspects of their event. The SAG should not be considered as a threatening environment as the safety of all involved in an event should be mutually beneficial.

The SAG should not make unreasonable or unfair demands on the organiser and the options highlighted in section 3.8 under 'smarter working' should be considered. These include technological solutions such as video/teleconferencing. The SAG should also guard against placing disproportionate demands on organisers of what are obviously very low-risk events.

Wherever possible SAGs should still seek to assess the safety arrangements of an event, despite such a lack of participation by an organiser. It should also then address any issues raised by the most appropriate means. It will be particularly important to ensure that accurate and appropriate records of representations and correspondence are maintained in these situations.

In any case, the SAG chair should coordinate its members' desires and attempts to communicate with the organiser, ensuring that attempts are recorded and properly documented.

D.3   What can be done where an event organiser does not accept the advice of the SAG?

The SAG is purely an advisory body and as such an organiser may feel justified in ignoring its advice. However, if it is the case that the SAG comprises competent individuals from the relevant organisations, there must be real doubts about the wisdom of ignoring such advice.

It may well be that a member of the SAG will consider the use of statutory powers, where it is felt that public safety would be compromised. It is important to stress that such action would be a matter for that member's organisation and not for the SAG.

It is equally important to stress that the event organiser (and its contractors) has the duty to manage risk and take any appropriate action – not the SAG.

D.4 Is there a potential conflict of interest when certain agencies on a SAG are also responsible for enforcement?

The possibility that enforcement action could result in respect of any event organiser or venue cannot be ignored. Clearly this could apply to licensing, safety certification, criminal or fire safety-related matters. However, this should not preclude participation in a SAG as the advantage of this far outweighs suggestions of conflict of interest.

Experience has shown that in the vast majority of cases any potential safety concerns can be resolved informally, with the SAG often playing a pivotal part. Other options in the case of sports grounds could include the review of safety certificates and prohibition notices.

D.5 Should the SAG be a part of the event planning process?

As stressed at various stages in this guidance, the SAG processes are about the quality assurance of safety arrangements including the event documentation. Terms of reference sometimes suggest 'advise and assist event organisers'. While 'advise' will be an appropriate term SAGs should exercise caution of the use of 'assist'. Particularly where there may be a well-developed relationship with an event organiser, there are occasions where SAGs exceed their advisory remit in favour of recommending how concerns and safety issues can be resolved.

In such a case it is necessary to consider whether this may transfer a degree of liability from the event organiser, or venue, to the SAG or member in question.

This should not prevent the SAG or its members sharing local knowledge and previous event good practice with organisers through the SAG process. Failure to do so would fall short of government's desire to encourage events, and indeed, potentially the SAG's own objectives to encourage events to be as safe as practicable.

D.6 Can an event planner and/or manager be a member of the SAG?

There is nothing to preclude this, although some caution should be exercised where members may be scrutinising their own plans. Ideally the planning and SAG representatives should be different people, although there may clearly be a requirement for 'planners' to attend the SAG during discussions relative to their documentation.

Members of a SAG may also be a part of the event management structure, and again there is nothing to preclude this. It is, however, good practice to ensure that there are clearly documented distinctions between planning, SAG and management forums.

Furthermore it is essential to ensure that there is a clear timeline to distinguish when a SAG advisory function for an event is superseded by the event management group.

D.7   Should the SAG inspect a venue and event site?

As a SAG has no statutory powers use of the phrase 'inspection' is to be avoided as this implies the potential for enforcement action. It is, however, good practice for SAG members to be familiar with venues and events in order to discharge their roles effectively within the SAG. We would prefer to call these familiarisation visits and not inspections.

D.8   Should the SAG be involved in the debriefing for an event?

The debriefing of events is a crucial aspect of learning for the future of that and other events (as noted in *Review of Persistent Lessons Identified Relating to Interoperability from Emergencies and Major Incidents Since 1986*).[7] The SAG should always encourage the event organisers to undertake a debriefing process, although the SAG is probably not the right place to undertake this. The debriefing process may well highlight lessons for the SAG itself in terms of its processes and procedures.

D.9   Can a SAG apply conditions to an event?

In short the answer is no, a SAG itself has no authority *per se*. However, it is not unusual for the SAG to make safety recommendations to a licensing authority that could impact upon the determination of such conditions. Certainly the SAG should not be considered as a pressure group to apply undue influence on the licensing authority in relation to such conditions.

D.10   Does involvement in a SAG make its members or their organisation 'responsible' for the event?

One reason for not establishing, or sometimes not attending, a SAG has been that by doing so the agency in question could be culpable in the event of a safety-related incident occurring at an event subject to the SAG processes.

While it may be understandable that this view exists, the contrary should also be considered. If an event led to injury, or worse, and it was established that an agency had any 'duty of care', or any responsibility to scrutinise event arrangements, then it could be equally culpable for having failed to do so.

Such considerations should always be taken in the light of legal advice from the agency's own department.

D.11   What should the SAG do if it is asked to consider matters of public safety that fall outside the knowledge and experience of its members?

One option available to the SAG is to delay consideration of the matter until such time as it can secure the necessary expertise within its member groups. If this is still not possible, and assuming it is a SAG role and is necessary, it may consider obtaining that advice externally through consultants or other agencies where the expertise does lie. This will, of course, incur costs, although if justifiable, these might be transferable to the organiser (see question D.12 below).

D.12   What funding is available for a SAG?

It is possible that a SAG may need to fund some exceptional situation, such as a requirement for specialist or technical advice. It is unlikely that a SAG will have a budget but, where possible, it would be appropriate to approach an event organiser or venue for such support. Of course there is no legal obligation for them to do so.

Alternatively it may fall to member organisations to reach agreement over how such costs may be covered, where such advice is necessary to ensure the group is able to effectively scrutinise the safety arrangements for the event.

D.13 What if the event crosses town, borough or other administrative borders?

Such events are not uncommon and many have taken place around the UK in recent years. The Olympic Torch Relay and Tour de France are two such examples, but many more have occurred. In such instances it is essential that early agreement is obtained between the various potential SAGs that might be involved to agree a common approach and, if necessary, to merge the SAGs for the specific event. All parties will have to agree that divergent opinions will occur and that negotiating common ground will be the most important task for the chair(s) to achieve.

D.14 Should the SAG consider aspects of an event such as disability issues, lost and found children, etc.?

There is a fine line to be drawn here and the focus must be on safety. It would not be a role for the SAG to consider arrangements under the Disability Act or the Equalities Act 2010. However, this should be a consideration where matters of egress and evacuation are concerned. For instance, the height or location of a wheelchair viewing platform would not be a matter for SAG, but if it were placed without adequate means of escape, it should certainly consider it.

Missing children and vulnerable adults are potentially a matter of public safety and as such the SAG may wish to satisfy itself that adequate measures are in place.

D.15 Should a SAG raise safety concerns with an event organiser's insurers?

While employment liability policies are mandatory it is important to recognise that there is no legal requirement for an event organiser to obtain public liability insurance, nor can a SAG demand that a certificate of insurance be produced for examination. For smaller, less complex events, it is common to have a combined policy that has been obtained by an organiser online. For larger and more complex events a broker or underwriter may be involved given the greater scrutiny and detail that would be necessary to assess the insured risks.

In extreme cases some SAGs have written to insurers to outline their safety concerns. However, to some degree insurers are unlikely to wish to get involved in such matters as issues of confidentiality could be involved that would not be disclosable to a third party. It must also be considered that this could result in the unwelcome outcome of an insurer withdrawing cover, causing an event to go ahead without insurance.

If a broker or underwriter is involved it will act in the interests of both the insurer and event organiser. As such it may well be that it will be in a position to influence actions to address such safety concerns.

Appendix E   About this guidance

E.1   How it came about

The Emergency Planning College (epc) Crowd and Public Safety Faculty has for many years led in this area with numerous courses, especially 'Working in Safety Advisory Groups', which is supported by the SGSA, formerly the Football Licensing Authority (FLA). This course has been delivered around the UK and has captured many opinions and issues, and, alongside work supporting government departments, professional groups, etc. it has led to the faculty being asked to provide this guidance.

The faculty was provided with research from the industry (by Eric Stuart, Queen's Police Medal (QPM), an associate epc and crowd safety advisor), which also showed a need for guidance in this area. This in turn led to wider research and discussion with public organisations and professional groups within the events industry. A review of other guidance in this area was made, and two relevant documents were identified. The first was prepared by The Core Cities Group and the second by the Chartered Institute of Environmental Health (CIEH) for the Olympics in 2012, as listed in Appendix G. The CIEH had been proposing to produce a second version of its guidance, but was happy to support the production of this guidance instead.

E.2   Development

Having completed the research, the epc sought a core consultation group from the sports, event industries and public services, including those who scrutinise and examine event arrangements through statutory processes, to work on the outline of the guidance and complete the initial consultation. The members of core consultation group are listed below. While this work was commencing, the Events Industry Forum (EIF) was finalising its rewrite of the *Event Safety Guide* as the *Purple Guide*,[1] and it was agreed that the epc would also write the chapter on Safety Advisory Groups. This guidance, then, is written in conjunction with the *Purple Guide* chapter on working with a Safety Advisory Group. The initial consultation issues were taken on board and then went to a general consultation, before the guidance was produced in its final format.

E.3   Consultation process group

The following professional groups and organisations were represented during the core consultation process:

Association of Chief Police Officers
Association of Event Venues
Association of Festival Organisers
Association of Independent Festivals
Basingstoke and Deane Borough Council
Britain for Events Campaign
Cabinet Office
Chartered Institute of Environmental Health
Chartered Institute for the Management of Sport and Physical Activity
Chief Fire Officers' Event Safety Group
College of Policing
Core Cites Group
Department for Communities and Local Government

Durham Council
Earls Court and Olympia Venues
Events Industry Forum
Football Safety Officers' Association
Hanover Communications
Health and Safety Executive
Horsey Lightly Fynn Solicitors
Institute of Entertainment and Arts Management
Institute of Event Management
Institute of Occupational Safety and Health
Local Authority Event Organisers' Group
Local Government Association
National Outdoor Event Association
NEC Group
Nottinghamshire Police
Production Services Association
Royal Environmental Health Institute of Scotland
Safety Advisors' Group in Entertainment
Safer Communities Resilience Division, Scottish Government
Showmen's Guild
Sports Ground Safety Authority
Superact

E.4   Guidance

It is intended that this guidance should be used by all involved with safety at events; it hopes to bring the clarity and consistency that was sought. It was written and scrutinised by those in the industry for the benefit of those who work in or are new to the industry, and organisations that advise and support events.

E.5   In future

It is intended that this guidance will be reviewed annually, for possible future versions, and it will be utilised on the epc's course on 'Working in Safety Advisory Groups'. The faculty will continue to work with events industry professional groups and to partner with other organisations and agencies.

The guidance will continue to inform the *Purple Guide*[1] chapter on working with Safety Advisory Groups.

The initial core consultation group discussed whether the guidance should be submitted through the processes of obtaining British Standards Institution certification. This will be considered with future reviews and industry support.

Appendix F   Glossary

Category 1 responder
An agency such as a fire, police and ambulance service, with responsibilities under the Civil Contingencies Act.

Dreamspace
An art structure built in a park at Chester-Le-Street in 2006 that was lifted by winds and led to the deaths of two people and injury to many others.

epc
The Cabinet Office Emergency Planning College where courses are run on 'Public safety' and 'Working in Safety Advisory Groups' as well as on contingency planning and disaster management.

FLA
The Football Licensing Authority, predecessor of the Sports Grounds Safety Authority.

FTP
File transfer protocols – a means of sharing data and large files via secure online storage systems.

Green Guide
The informal title for the *Guide to Safety at Sports Grounds*.[4] This publication was first developed after the Ibrox disaster and is maintained by the SGSA. It is used primarily at sports grounds, although it does give some help in relation to crowd flows and densities for event planners.

JESIP
The Joint Emergency Services Interoperability Programme. A programme introduced by government to improve the planning and response to major incidents across the UK.

Method statement
A document that explains safe systems of work and applies primarily to the construction industry, although it is becoming more common elsewhere.

Monsters of Rock
A music concert held annually at Donington Park where two fatalities occurred in 1988.

Policy
An underpinning, guiding principle (or principles) on which terms of reference can be based.

Pop Code
In this context, the forerunner to the *Purple Guide*;[1] not to be confused with HSE guidance on noise at festivals.

Purple Guide
The Purple Guide to Health, Safety and Welfare at Music and Other Events[1] is the well-known guide to health, safety and welfare at events. This was originally an HSE document (*HSG195 The Event Safety Guide*); the new version was written by professionals within the industry.

SAG

Safety Advisory Group. Sometimes known as ESAG (Event Safety Advisory Group), PSAG (Public Safety Advisory Group) PESAG (Public Event Safety Advisory Group), LSAG (Licensing Safety Advisory Group) or it could be prefixed by the name of a county or town.

SGSA

Sports Ground Safety Authority, formally known as the Football Licensing Authority (FLA).

Temporary demountable structures

Items designed to be built and rebuilt on a regular basis and for relatively short periods of time at event and festival sites. These will include stages, marquees, seating areas, platforms and floodlights.

Terms of reference

An agreed list of what the SAG is intended to achieve and what it will (or will not) do.

Third-party review

Any process by which an individual or group not involved in the process undertakes an examination of the processes or documentation. Peer review and external review would be included in this process.

Tribute events

These are arranged (often at short notice) to commemorate significant incidents, often deaths of significant personalities or to raise the public profile of some form of major campaign (for example, Children in Need).

Triggers

A list of risk-based factors upon which the SAG may decide whether to meet and/or consider the safety aspects of certain events.

Appendix G   References, further reading and further guidance

G.1   References

1. *The Purple Guide to Health, Safety and Welfare at Music and Other Events.* Entertainment Industry Forum, March 2014. This is an important document used by event-related organisers and scrutinisers of events. It supersedes *HSG195 The Event Safety Guide.* It is the core document for most people working within the outdoor events and music industry. It has to be noted, however, that it is only a guide and like all such documents it is not for strict adherence but relies on the expertise of those in the industry applying its principles to a given set of circumstances. Purchase of the document can only be made online after registration and payment of an annual fee of £25. It is available at:

   http://www.thepurpleguide.co.uk/

2. *Report of the Inquiry into Crowd Safety at Sports Grounds.* Rt Hon Lord Wheatley. Her Majesty's Stationery Office, 1972.

3. *The Hillsborough Stadium Disaster 15 April 1989. Final Report.* Home Office and Rt Hon Lord Justice Taylor. Her Majesty's Stationery Office, January 1990. Available at:

   http://www.epcollege.com/EPC/media/MediaLibrary/Knowledge%20Hub%20Document s/F%20Inquiry%20Reports/Hillsborough-Taylor-Report.pdf?ext=.pdf

4. *Guide to Safety at Sports Grounds (The Green Guide).* Sports Ground Safety Authority (SGSA) on behalf of the Department for Culture, Media and Sport, fifth edition, 2008. This is the distillation of many years of research and experience of the safety management and design of sports grounds. It is available from TSO at:

   http://www.tsoshop.co.uk/bookstore.asp?Action=Book&ProductId=0117020745

   A downloadable version is available from SGSA at:

   http://www.safetyatsportsgrounds.org.uk/sites/default/files/publications/green-guide.pdf

5. *Live Music Exchange*, April 2010. Available at:

   http://livemusicexchange.org/resources/a-report-on-the-size-and-value-of-britains-events-industry-its-characteristics-trends-opportunities-and-key-issues/

6. *Organising a Voluntary Event: A 'Can Do' Guide.* Cabinet Office, January 2014. Central government has circulated this guidance to the organisers of voluntary and community based events. The title is indicative of this approach and the content is strongly supportive of organisers. This is available at:

   https://www.gov.uk/government/publications/can-do-guide-for-organisers-of-voluntary-events/the-can-do-guide-to-organising-and-running-voluntary-and-community-events

It is also important to note the government's desire for local authorities and other agencies to be supportive and helpful towards event organisers, citing previous guidance as 'too heavily focused upon why events could not, or should not proceed'. The guide makes no reference to SAGs but it is important to stress the restricted nature of the occasions it is aimed at, i.e. voluntary and community events.

7. *Review of Persistent Lessons Identified Relating to Interoperability from Emergencies and Major Incidents Since 1986. Occasional Papers New Series Number 6.* Emergency Planning College, 2013. It is noted that lessons have not been learned from the events to the extent that there is sufficient change in both policy and practice to prevent their repetition. This publication is available at:

http://www.jesip.org.uk/wp-content/uploads/2013/07/Pollock-Review-Oct-2013.pdf

G.2 Further reading

Fire Safety Risk Assessments. Department for Communities and Local Government, first published 2012. Various titles in this series are relevant but especially *Open-Air Events and Venues, Large Places of Assembly, Small and Medium Places of Assembly* and *Means of Escape for Disabled People.* All of these guides give useful advice for event organisers and those undertaking scrutiny or enforcement roles at events although such scrutiny should, wherever possible, be undertaken by qualified and experienced fire officers. Bespoke guidance is also available for Scotland. The guides are available at:

https://www.gov.uk/government/collections/fire-safety-law-and-guidance-documents-for-business

Guide to the Safety Certification of Sports Grounds. Sports Grounds Safety Authority, 2009. This supersedes the guidance on safety certification issued by the Football Licensing Authority in 2001. This is available at:

http://www.safetyatsportsgrounds.org.uk/sites/default/files/publications/safety-certification-guidance.pdf

HSG154 Managing Crowds Safely. Health and Safety Executive, 2014. The advice in this document is a good starting point as a referral document to crowd safety management. It is available online or can be purchased at:

http://www.hse.gov.uk/pubns/books/hsg154.htm

Safety Advisory Groups and Event Planning: Supporting the Environmental Health Contribution. Chartered Institute of Environment Health, November 2010. This was prepared for the 2012 Olympics but is still valid and is available at:

http://www.cieh.org/uploadedFiles/Core/Policy/2012_Olympics_and_Paralympics/Olympics_SAG_discussion_paper_FINAL.pdf

The Northern Ireland Guide to Safety at Sports Grounds (The Red Guide). Department of Culture, Arts and Leisure, 2007. This bespoke document is based upon the fourth edition of the *Green Guide.* The guide is not available online but can be purchased at:

http://www.tsoshop.co.uk/bookstore.asp?FO=1159966&Action=Book&ProductID=9780 337088711&From=SearchResults

Public Safety in Complex and Built Environments. Cabinet Office, 2007. This document introduces the concept of integrated safety management in the design and daily operations of these environments and is available at:

https://www.gov.uk/government/publications/public-safety-in-complex-and-built-environments

The Regulators' Code 2014. Better Regulation Delivery Office, 2014. This document is aimed at those with regulatory duties and will apply to many individual members of SAGs, although not to SAGs as a whole. Specifically it states that 'Regulators should carry out their activities in a way that supports those they regulate to develop and grow'. This is available at:

https://www.gov.uk/government/publications/regulators-code

Safety Guidance for Street Arts, Carnival Processions and Large-Scale Performances. ISAN, 2009. This is a short guide for inexperienced and intermediate event organisers and is available at:

http://isanuk.ohttp://www.isanuk.org/product/safety-guidance-for-street-arts-carnival-processions-and-large-scale-performance/rg/publications

Safety Management. Football Licensing Authority (now SGSA), 2009. This is a guide to safety procedures at sports grounds and makes reference (albeit briefly) to the role of SAGs. Again the document is not available online but can be purchased at:

http://www.safetyatsportsgrounds.org.uk/publications/safety-management

Understanding Crowd Behaviours. Emergency Planning College and Leeds University, 2010. This document is in two volumes and is available to purchase from TSO at:

http://www.tsoshop.co.uk/bookstore.asp?Action=Book&ProductId=9780114302054

It is also available as a download in five parts: *A Guide for Readers; Guidance and Lessons Identified; Supporting Evidence; Simulation Tools;* and *Supporting Documentation. Guidance and Lessons Identified* is a particularly useful part of this comprehensive piece of research, which includes findings that combined academic study with the knowledge of highly experienced event practitioners to produce a detailed study of crowd behaviours and strategies to predict and deal with these. These are available at:

https://www.gov.uk/government/publications/understanding-crowd-behaviours-documents

G.3   Other guidance
Health and Safety Executive
Advice on the role of a local authority Safety Advisory Group is available on the HSE website at: http://www.hse.gov.uk/event-safety/safety-advisory-Groups.htm

The Core Cities Group

The Core Cities Group issued comprehensive guidance some years ago that remains useful today. Although no longer available on the Core Cities Group website, a link remains on the Licensing Lawyers website. This is available at:

http://www.licensinglawyers.co.uk/cms/safety-advisory-Groups/

Joint Emergency Services Interoperability Programme

The Joint Emergency Services Interoperability Programme (JESIP) is the UK government's response to try to ensure that emergency services respond to major incidents and events in a more coordinated fashion. Although it is not relevant to most event organisers, its products and practices will become core methods of responding, and therefore planning, for major incidents and as such, knowledge of these might be of use to partners and external companies who will meet in the SAG context. Guidance is available at:

http://www.jesip.org.uk/